Help Me Be Good

Whining

Joy Berry
Illustrated by Bartholomew

Joy Berry Books
New York

This book is about Annie.

Reading about Annie can help you understand and deal with whining.

Whining is crying or talking in a complaining, nagging way.

Have you ever been with someone who is whining?

When you are with someone who is whining, how do you feel?

What do you think?

What do you do?

When you are with someone who is whining, you might get upset.

You might decide you do not want to be with the person.

There are several reasons why you might whine.

You might whine because things are not happening the way you want them to happen.

Your parents might tell you "no" or ask you to do something you do not want to do.

You might whine to get them to change their minds and let you have your own way.

But whining will only make things worse.

Do not whine when you do not get your way.

Do these things instead:
- Remember that you cannot have your own way all the time.
- Tell your parents politely how you feel. Give them time to think about what you say. What you say might cause them to change their minds. If it does not, stop talking about it.

You might whine because you want attention.

You might want your parents to notice you or spend some time with you.

But whining will not get you the kind of attention you want or need.

Do not whine when you want attention.

Do these things instead:
- Tell your parents politely that you need some attention.
- Plan a time when they can spend time with you. Wait for that time. Do not bother them while you wait.

You might whine because you are bored.

You might not have anything to do.

You might think whining will get your parents to entertain you.

But whining will only make things worse.

Do not whine when you are bored.

Do these things instead:
- Remember that it is your job to keep yourself busy. It is not up to anyone else to entertain you.
- Tell your parents politely that you are bored. Ask them to suggest things for you to do.
- If you do not like any of their suggestions, you need to choose some things you can do. Be sure to get permission to do whatever you decide to do.

You might whine because you are hungry, tired, or sick. You might become cranky when your body needs something or when you are not feeling well.

Do not whine when you are hungry, tired, or sick.

Do these things instead:
- Eat some food if you are hungry.
- Get some rest if you are tired.
- Do the things you need to do to get well if you are sick.

You might whine because it is a habit. A habit is something you do so often or for so long that you do it without thinking.

Ask the people around you to help you break the habit of whining.

Ask them to tell you when you are whining.

Stop immediately when they let you know that you are whining.

Continue to do this until you do not whine anymore.

Your parents might need to do one of two things when you whine:

- They might need to ignore you. This does not mean that they don't love you. They might ignore you because they want you to learn that whining is not a good way for you to get attention.
- They might need to walk away from you or send you to another room. This does not mean that they don't love you. It is what they might need to do so that your whining does not upset them or other people.

It is important to treat other people the way you want to be treated.

If you do not want people to whine around you, you must not whine around them.

Joy Berry Enterprises
146 West 29th St., Suite 11RW
New York, NY 10001

Cover Design & Art Direction: John Bellaud
Cover Illustration & Art Production: Geoff Glisson

Production Location: HX Printing, Guangzhou, China
Date of Production: February 2010
Cohort: Batch 1

Printed in China
ISBN 978-1-60577-134-2